The Ring of Azurmus

By the Same Author

Love's Dawn

Gaze the Moon

The Ring

of

Azurmus

Andrew Chiniche

Reflective
Light
Press

The Ring of Azurmus by Andrew Chiniche

Published by Reflective Light Press
Copyright © 2020 Andrew Chiniche

First Edition: April 2020
Printed in the United States of America

Library of Congress Control Number: 2020904622

Paperback ISBN: 978-1-7326824-7-4
Hardback ISBN: 978-1-7326824-8-1

Edited by Eva Zen
Cover by Manuela Serra

Part 1

The Magician

THE MAGICIAN.

I hold the parchment
with ink-stained fingers
and scratch the quill
across its surface.

Words bubble from my soul
and deposit themselves upon the page.
I write in celebration of my muse,
the source of my creativity.

I describe my overwhelming love for her
and the unstoppable perfection of her beauty.
She deserves worship and her own religion.

From the depths of my being,
I sacrifice my essence
as an offering to her.

After folding this sacred document into thirds,
I drip ruby wax from a burning taper
to seal the message inside.

Turning in my chair,
away from the desk,
I call my squire.
"Boy!

Take this missive
and deliver it to the
Keep of Our Triple Mother."

"Do...
Do you mean the witches,
my Lord?"

"Yes.
You better leave now
or you will be trapped
in the fall of night
and devoured as their meal."

"As you wish,
my Lord."

Leaning back in my chair,
I watch the frightened lad leave
with my letter of devotion.

I know my lady love will not harm him,
but he must learn not to falsely judge others
from rumors and aspersions.

I grab the nearby goblet,
swirl the remaining imperial nectar,
and wash it down my gullet.

Memories of our first rendezvous
dance through my mind.

Two

At the stroke of midnight,
I enter the Society's gala
and see her shimmer in the crowd,
her face hidden behind an intricate mask.

Sea-foam feathers plume around
her frozen porcelain features
with lips formed into a forever pout.

Bright golden eyes drive a spike
into my heart and capture me.
The surrounding sea of people disappears
as we slip into another dimension.

With outstretched arms,
she beckons me into her embrace.
I am drawn towards her
and want to discover her mystery.

Through a gown of sparkling darkness,
I feel her muscles coil, taut and ready to strike.

Her muffled voice hums through the mask.
"The time of the Convergence has arrived.
Search for the Talisman and you shall find me."

As the final bell of the grandfather clock peals,
vibrating my eardrums,
the crowd reemerges around us.

She releases me and drifts away,
disappearing into the room.

In the space of twelve seconds,
my life derails and I transform.
A new destination and goal absorb my mind.

To escape the crush of people,
I retreat through a pair of French doors
and exit onto a balcony.

As I overlook a rapidly flowing river,
it crests into a waterfall.

I breathe deep of the crisp night air
and gather my thoughts—
I must discover who she is.

After some time, I reenter the party
and spend the rest of the night

conversing, chatting, and laughing
in the pretense of enjoying myself.

Deep inside, I know she has left,
but I continue to watch for her anyway.

Before dawn peeks its way above the horizon,
I have the house footman bring my carriage around.

I travel home
to put my weary thoughts
and body to bed.

Sleeping through the internal buzz of alcohol,
I have a vision of her.

Transfixing me with a gaze of the sun,
she places both hands on the sides
of her mask and lifts it from her face.

After a quick release,
the porcelain plummets to the floor
and explodes upon impact.
The shards scatter to eternity.

She is a universe of stars
with a black hole for a mouth.

As her lips part,
I feel the pull of gravity
draw me into her orbit.

Comets fly across her face
as her words bounce around my mind.

**"Impale yourself on the Spear of Desire
and bring me the Chalice of Life.
Only then you shall be worthy and free."**

Awakening with a quake,
I lay in a shallow pool of sweat.

The low winter sun has
reached its afternoon peak
and shines through my window,
bathing me in a heated light.

Fumbling for the bell-pull,
I call a servant into my room.

"Did you ring, Sir?"

"Y-yes... yes.
Pour me a tonic and prepare my bath.
I am in need of a soothing soak."

"As you wish,
my Lord."

Submerging myself in a steaming tub
does me a world of good
and goes a long way to clearing my head.

I soak long enough for my fingers
and toes to wrinkle into raisins.

As my bath reaches the surrounding air temperature,
I feel a chill and decide to exit.

Grabbing the brass railing
attached to the wall,
I hoist myself to my feet.

Taking a cashmere towel in hand,
I quickly whisk away the wet residue
and slide into a silk dragon robe
procured from my tour of the Far East.

As I exit the washroom,
leaving wet prints fading behind me,
I pad down the hallway
and enter my private office.

Nestled in an oversized nook,
a great mahogany desk
is surrounded by a bay window.

It overlooks the winding meadow
at the back of the estate.

A pair of deer, a buck and a doe, prance past
and seem to look at me through the glass.

Turning away from the outside nature,
I open a large drawer towards the bottom of the desk.

I remove my bottle of thirty-year scotch
while clicking a hidden latch
with my right hand.

A small trap door creaks to reveal my grimoire.

With a cover bound in human flesh
and worn smooth by the progression of time,
this book has been in my possession
since I began my magickal journey.

When I came of age, my mentor completed
the cycle of my training by presenting it to me.

Although it appears full of writings,
there will always be a blank page.

Armed with the bottle of liquid courage,
I tuck the book of spells into my robe's sash
and make my way to an interior wall.

With a supple hand,
I reach for a lever hidden in the bookcase
and pull it down with a click.

An entrance to a secret passage
swings open and I slink in.

Once an ancient priest-hole,
it leads to a narrow staircase
carved from granite.

Candlelight guides my way
as the scotch glows amber in its decanter.

I have traveled this way many times
and could walk it in my sleep.

At the bottom of the stairs,
the passage opens into a chamber.

I can hear water dripping from the ceiling
and feel a glove of humidity surround me.

As I walk down the aisle,
I light a number of tapers.

A soft yellow glow fills the room.

Underneath an inverted cross,
an altar cut from black alabaster
patiently waits for me.

After placing the decanter on the altar,
I lay my tome on a beautifully wrought iron stand
and open it to a passage about dream fulfillment.

"Father below,
bringer of night.

I call to you
for what is right.

Drag my dreams
to the light.

Help me to expose
the strength of their might."

I grab an earthenware cup,
place it next to the stand,
and take a small sharpened stake in hand.

I grit my teeth as the point drags across
my palm, bringing blood to the surface.

As I slowly pour scotch over my cupped hand,
it washes the wound and flows into the vessel.

"As my blood
mixes with spirits,
I offer you pain
and give you fire."

I place my hand directly into the flame
and my alcohol-soaked skin ignites.

"As you burn below,
I burn with you.
I ask for knowledge
as the flames turn to blue."

The liquid burns off
and the flames dissipate,
leaving scorch marks.

I swirl the bloody scotch mixture
around three times,
close my eyes, and drink.

"Follow the darkened full moon
to the beginning of morning.
Only then shall the way open to you.

Do not let desire destroy you.
The Chalice must remain pure."

I awake on the floor,
clammy from the surrounding
moldy dampness.

I pull myself together,
gather my belongings,
and return up the stairs.

As I close the desk's bottom drawer,
its contents returned,
I look out the bay window.
The waxing crescent glares at me.

I have fourteen days to prepare
until the moon reaches its complete fullness,
the coming of the lunar eclipse,
and the beginning of my quest.

Three

As the full moon dawns
and the sun finishes its daily descent,
I am ready to begin my journey.

Dressed in a leather jerkin
with a light knapsack,
I carry a staff hewn
from a birch branch.
It is blessed in the ritual of traveling.

Moccasins hug my feet to ensure a safe grip.
I set my sights on the shimmering orb
and begin walking, humming a tune.

Minutes grow into hours,
and I feel a burn in my muscles
as the pathway ascends at a steady incline.

With the celestial lantern as my guide,
the stars disappear and the dark sky
blacks out the landscape.

The inkiness of night leaks onto the moon
and the eclipse flows with a smooth crescent edge.

As I climb ghost steps leading into the nether realm,
all my focus absorbs in the darkening sphere.

Brimstone burns my nostrils.
The forest of suicides wafts
its despair over my psyche
and I feel soul-crushing loneliness.

Sweat beads on my brow
and drips into my eyes
with a stinging saltiness.
I must continue to press forward.

The satellite becomes completely blotted out,
a brighter darkness in the midnight sky.

My ordeal is halfway complete.

A sliver of light appears
at the bottom of the moon
as the eclipse moves from full.

Shooting across the sky
and cutting its way through the mist,
a Roman road composed
of photons appears before me.

Stepping from the earth onto this new pathway,
I am whisked away and transported to a desolate field
where a veiny pulsating Carnal Tower dwarfs me.

The smell of spent musk
and desperate couplings
fills my sinuses.

As I fight to push myself forward,
my feet sink into the muddy muck.

The opposing structure draws me towards it.

The door to the tower cracks open
and a moan of used passion
echoes in my ears.

A beast of unbridled lust bursts out
of the entrance before me.

With a muscular hermaphroditic body,
carrying a large phallic shape spear,
its face twists like that of a scorned lover.

In the center of my mind,
a seductive voice speaks.

"I am Yssup.
It is my duty to guard the burning ardor
of the Forgotten Kingdom.
What brings you uninvited to my realm?"

"I am Lord Edwin,
Master of the Dark Arts
and Keeper of the Forbidden Language.

With the full moon as my guide,
my quest led me through the eclipse
and has brought me here.

I seek the Talisman.

Will you allow me safe passage?"

"None may pass.
Retreat now
or I shall repel you."

The majestic sphere has set,
leaving a non-light to fill the area.
My path of entry had disappeared.

The beast glares at me
and levels his spear in my direction;
it seems to harden and elongate.

"Surrender to him.
She will take you into the tower,
where you shall discover the chalice."

I kneel on the ground, bow my head,
and lay my walking stick down.

"Guardian of hideous strength.
Pray grant me your forgiveness.
My intention was not to intrude upon your realm.
I surrender to your custody."

Yssup trudges towards me
and positions herself behind my back.

I hear a grunting roar followed by a sharp pain
as he strikes the back of my head.

The desolate field and the Carnal Tower
fade to blackness with the shuttering of my eyes.

As I awaken with a throbbing head,
the smell of wet straw fills my nose
and a thin warmth covers me.

A coarse moth-eaten blanket
itches my naked skin.

The remnants of an unremembered meal
and a dirty glass containing an amber liquid
rests on a side table.

The surrounding stone room
is bare of furnishings except for
an overstuffed chair by the window.

My clothing waits neatly folded on top of my knapsack
and my walking stick rests along the wall.

A near-silent sobbing bounces
around the room from the outside corridor
through a wooden panel door.

As I move to a sitting position,
the bed's timbers creak
with my body's shifting weight.

Light swims around my eyes
in unison with the beating of my brain.

I probe the welt on the back
of my head with unsure fingers.
A shock of pain travels throughout my nerve endings.

Since I feel too wobbly to walk,
I get on all fours and crawl towards my wardrobe.

As I lean against the wall and dress,
a darkened shadows hovers, which is visible through
the space between the floor and door.

With a rattle of the handle
and squeak of rusty hinges,
the wooden barrier pushes inward.

I am temporarily hidden
on the side attached to the wall.

Willing myself quiet and sitting immobile,
I watch as a being enters the chamber
and walks towards my bed,
carrying a tray covered with a white cloth.

The smell of hot food,
fresh and filling,
causes my mouth to water.

I see before me a maiden
with long, flowing blonde tresses
and a shapely figure.

Taking a chance,
I call out.
 "Miss.
Who are you
and what do you bring?"

After gasping
and almost dropping her burden,
she turns to face me.

"I see that you have recovered sufficiently
to remove yourself from bed.

You may call me Alice.
I too am a prisoner of Yssup.

Here. Let us get you back under the cover."

She places the tray on the floor
and helps me back to where I started.

"You are well met, Alice.
I thank you for your attention
to my well-being.

I am Edwin, a wayward traveler.
How did you come here?"

"I was kidnapped by Yssup
from the home of my sister,
The Keep of Our Triple Mother,
and brought here to this non-place:
a realm of spent seed and forbidden passions."

As she speaks,
her oval face is framed
by the draping of flaxen locks.

I can see the raging
of a summer ocean simmer
around the pupils of her eyes.

Unconsciously, she holds my hand
in hers during the unfurling of her tale.
I feel the stirrings of desire bubble deep within me.

"When I take my leave of this place,
I will bring you with me.
You have my pledge."

"Let us not speak of that now.
The cycle of the day is ending.
I will visit you on the morrow
and we will explore the situation."

I wait with baited breath
as I watch the sun's beam travel
along the floor in its morning progression.

I feel stronger in mind and body.
The time of rest has gone a long way
to reviving my energy.

The screaming hinges
announce her arrival.

She is transitioning from childhood
and growing into a woman.

There is a fluid innocence about her
that skates on the edge of sensuality.
She does not yet realize her beauty
or the power of her sexuality.

The seed of desire planted inside me
elongates and sharpens into a spear
that pierces through my body.

With an involuntary reaction,
my flesh engorges full of blood
and grows hard in lust.

I love the way her robe clings
with a greedy grip to her body.

I want to have her,
but I must fight my inclination.

As she moves closer,
I try to hide my bulge with my arm.

"Good morning, Edwin.
I see that you are awake.
Let me take a look at your wound."

I tilt my head forward
as her fingers probe.
Her scent lingers around me.

She smells of newly blossomed roses
with a hint of honey.

A small giggle dances
through her lips.

"The swelling has gone down,
but I notice that it has increased elsewhere."
I say nothing,
but my cheeks glow a light crimson.

Alice sits on the edge of the bed,
and rests her hand on my arm.

We enjoy each other's company
and the sound of silence.

After a moments respite,
she hops up.

"Come, Lord Edwin.
T'is time to jump out of your recline
and into your clothes.

Yssup leaves during the day
and we can explore the tower
and this realm.

Do not be modest.
I will avert my eyes
to ease your mind."

Although she turns her back to me,
I can feel her glancing at my nakedness
as I work my way into my clothes.

After I am dressed,
she takes me by the hand.

"Come on.
Let's leave your room."

The doorway opens
into a spiral staircase
and she leads me.

We ascend the tower
passing various doors, some open,
most closed to trespassers.

"You seem to be free to travel at your whim.
What keeps you trapped here?"

"Yssup expects me to heed the directions
he imparted me with when she brought me here.
I live within the bounds of my honor."

As we spring up the steps,
the living energy of her body
is molten desire next to me.

She embodies grace
and style while affecting me
with her aura.

She catches my glances at her body,
stops us on a landing,
and whispers in my ear.

"If you're a good boy,
I will allow you to drink of my cup
and take my purity."

Startled,
I take a step back
and words of warning flood
into my mind.

"Do not let desire destroy you.
The Chalice must remain pure."

Alice is the Chalice
and the lynchpin in my search
for the Talisman.

I hold her at arm's length
and, with a serious expression,
look directly into her eyes.

"Alice.
Do you know of the Talisman
and its location?"

"Of course I do, silly.
I've always known.

Although I am young,
I contain the wisdom of the ancients
and the key to their secret arts."

I stare at her slack-jawed
as she continues.

"You must have been
sent here by my sister.
Watch for her.

She will consume you
and drink your soul."

Turning away from me,
she looks up the stairs
and resumes her climb.

Dumbfounded, I follow.

After reaching the top of the staircase,
I lift the beam holding the door shut
and let it lean against the wall.

The door drags as I push it open.

The roof is a flat expanse
with a small wall and a number of turrets
along the circle of the tower.

Alice skips around
humming a child's song
as I walk to the edge.

The blue cloudless sky
descends below the horizon.
Light surrounds us everywhere
but there is no sun.

A slight breeze smells of pine
as it drifts from the north
and feels of a distant chill.

The land disappears in the distance.
It seems like I can see further than it stretches.

"Alice.
Do you know where Yssup goes?"

"He is a traveler of the cardinal points.
Sometimes she searches where the sun is born
and sometimes he falls into its resting place.
To the south, she discovers the ancient seas,
and to the north, the lands of winter."

"You speak of the sun and its path
but look into the sky. It does not exist.
What kind of place is this realm?"

"That is not mine to speak of
and I shall not answer.

Edwin, you are not the
Keeper of the Forbidden Language.
You are the asker of many questions.

It is time for us to return to your chamber
and prepare for the coming of evening."

Alice whips away from me
and runs towards the stairs.

It is strange.
Although I know morning
was just recently upon us,
it feels as if an entire day has transpired.

I watch as the sky gains
the orangey colors of a setting sun.

I reach the doorway
and hear the clatter of her shoes
as she hurries down the tower.
She races beyond my field of vision.

I enter my chamber
and see dusk fall
across my window.

The wall sconces feed
a feeble yellow light
over the room.

My night's repast is set
close to my bed
on the side table.

Alice is nowhere to be found.

Once I'm finished eating,
I sit in the overstuffed chair
and think things over.

After some time,
I hear movement by my open door
and glance up.
It is Alice.

"Goodnight, Edwin.
I enjoyed our exploring this day.
I shall see you on the morrow."

Before I can utter a word in return,
she disappears
and leaves the door ajar.

Six

After tossing and turning
in a fitful sleep,
I sit upright in bed.

The darkness of night bleeds
through my window
and infects my room.

It is time for me to
explore on my own
without a guide.

Holding my walking stick
in front of me to feel my way,
I step gently in moccasin enclosed feet.

As I exit my room,
I notice the stairs
no longer lead up.

I walk in a spiral
until landing on the first floor.

I come upon an open door.
Peering inside
I see Alice covered
under a thin sheet.

The shadows thrown by the wall sconces
highlight the outline of her naked body.

She breaths heavily
as her chest heaves
and expands with air.

Low moans escape from her mouth.

Like Athena from Zeus' forehead,
the air begins to shimmer and grow
to form into a muscular creature
of a hideous beauty.

Before my eyes,
with his phallic spear
and her androgynous body,
Yssup appears!

As a distant echo in my head,
he speaks to me.

"Lord Edwin,
I know you are there.
Please enter.

I am the manifestation of
Alice's suppressed lust and desire.
She is the triple mother's aspect of purity
and must remain so.

Do you understand?"

I slowly nod.

"Tonight,
you will leave this realm
and take her with you

to continue your search
for the Talisman.

But first, you must come with me."

I step within reach of his arms
and take her extended hand.

"Close your eyes."

As I do so,
a whirlwind surrounds us
and a torrent of air buzzes
in my hearing.

After being lifted into the atmosphere,
I feel the soft caress of a cool breeze over my skin
and open my eyes.

We have been transported to an open field.
My clothes have disappeared and I am naked.

I crouch on my knees before Yssup.
He has a glorious erection
that pulsates before my face.
Her cunt drips below his shaft.

I understand what I must do.

I lean forward
and drink of the juices
that coat her meaty lips.

After I have swallowed my fill,
I wipe my mouth and run my tongue
along the veins of his cock.

As I reach her engorged head,
I open my mouth wide.
Yssup pushes himself down my throat.

Saliva runs over my chin
as I choke on the expanding mass.
I breathe rapidly through my nose
to gain oxygen.

She holds the sides
of my head to keep me steady.

Sliding out of my mouth,
he slaps her hardness on my cheeks
with an affectionate tap.

"Turn around."

Doing as I'm commanded,
I go one step further
and present my bottom for her use.

A barrage of lukewarm spittle coats my cheeks.
I feel Yssup's finger lube my hole.

My fists claw into the earth
and I clinch my teeth
as his throbbing spear of desire
forces its way inside me.

With each thrust,
there is a confusing mixture
of pleasure and pain.

A mask of shame burns on my cheeks
as excitement bubbles in my belly.

The thunderclaps of our slapping flesh
sounds across the sky
as my penis involuntary
hardens and drips pre-cum.

The world becomes intense,
lightning strikes across the universe,
and the earth quakes.

Yssup holds my hips tight
and bellows in triumph
with a final piercing gyration.

A geyser of lava erupts inside my lower half
and I slump face first into the ground.

Glancing up, I notice she has
started to fade, disappearing.

His corporal structure is no longer necessary
with the release of Alice's pent up lust and desire.

"Lord Edwin.
You have supped at my cup
and became the receptacle of my animus.
You have achieved the Chalice.

Take care of her.
You are her guardian
until she is delivered
unto her sister.

Sleep now and awake refreshed."

The echo in my head trails to a whisper
as Yssup completely disappears.

Everything goes dark
as my perception
of the world closes.

I awaken with the coming of morning

in between a spent campfire
and the road I began on.
The realm and the carnal tower are gone.

Across from me,
laying in the grass,
Alice sleeps in a restful pose
with a smile over her face.

Seven

"Hurry Edwin! We're almost there!"

Like a gazelle, Alice runs ahead
and causes me to give chase.

As I follow a trail of cast off clothing,
breathing hard and short of breath,
I catch up in time to watch her dive
with a flowing grace into a pool.

She surfaces for air,
motions for me to follow,
and swims towards a wall of wetness.

She disappears into a hidden opening.

I drop my nap-sack,
shuffle out of my outerwear,
and jump in.

A shock of coldness courses
throughout my body as I submerge.

Being a poor swimmer,
I dog paddle across
and travel underneath the waterfall.

As I reach a submerged rock ledge,
I crawl into the entrance of a cave.

The interior walls
coated with a translucency
glow with an internal light.

A sense of warmth radiates around me
and I hear a nervous giggle bounce
from deep inside the cave.

"Alice.
Are you ok?"

A grinding whisper returns to my ears.

"Yaassss.
Come follow meee."

THE EMPRESS.

A reflection of naked flesh
casts in the crystal walls.
Alice's face flows before me
with a look of erotic pleasure.

Crawling through the tunnel,
I follow the flow of air
that issues from the interior.

As I enter the antechamber,
I find Alice prostate before an alabaster slab.
A mumble of words pours from her lips.

The entire room is alive
with a rainbow light that pulsates
in unison to the rhythm of my heart.

Approaching the altar,
I am drawn to an open box at its center.

An oval-shaped stone,
like colors trapped in a water droplet,
is set in white metal
and suspended in a halo of diamonds.

I am captivated
by a cloud flowing
through its center.

As the mist parts,
I see three women
on the edge of a cliff.

The sky is electric around them
in exploding lighting.

A figure kneels before them in homage
and places an object
on the middle woman's finger.

A trembling of the earth
occurs in the vision
and the box snaps shut.

In tune with the quake I witnessed,
the cave vibrates around us,
pebbles and stones raining upon my head.

I scoop up the box in my left hand
and turn to collect Alice.
She has broken her trance
and stares at me from her prone position.

I herd her before me
and we hurry out of the deteriorating cave.

Exploding through the waterfall,
we splash into the pool
with a gangling leap.

Rolling onto my back,
I hold Alice as we float to shore.

As I gather up our scattered belongings,
the collapsed cave bellows a residue of dust.

Alice watches the sun set
through the canopy of trees
and I make our camp for the evening.

I open my prize
and remove it from its home.
The flames' light plays
in the interior of the main stone.

"Alice.
Do you know what this is?"

"Yes.
It is the Ring of Azurmus,
the Talisman."

Eight

The center stone, an Abyssinian opal,
was discovered on a journey by Mariam,
Queen of the Danakil Desert.

She was led to it through a dream.

After digging into the sharpened shale,
causing the skin of her hands
to hang in bloody tatters,
she removed the stone from the earth.

Her tears of pain were captured inside
the opal, causing the opaque stone
to have a translucent glow.

After traveling home,
she summoned the demon Azurmus
from the deepest pits to fashion
a setting to hold her find.

He pulled platinum from the dark side of the moon
and diamonds from the belly of a dying star.

To construct the ring,
he invented a pointed hammer
to pound the metal into shape.

After carefully setting the diamonds,
held invisibly by the ring's metal,
he mounted the opal in the center.

The spinning of the earth held still
and he was enraptured
with the beauty of what he had created.

He knew that he would not,
could not, give it away.

On the day of the presentation,
Azurmus brought Queen Mariam
her ring in an elaborate puzzle box.

Her thoughts became so entangled
in the dilemma before her
that she paid no heed to the demon.

Day turned into night,
and still the Queen worked
at opening the box.

As the sun rose,
with no one left in the banquet hall,
a loud click sounded and the lid sprang open.

With a gasp of delight,
she picked her ring out of the box
and slid it on.

As life blood traveled through
her ring finger to her heart,
Azurmus crept behind Mariam
with his pointed hammer in hand.

In a flash,
he raised it up
and with multiple downward swings
split her head open.

Mariam felt the pull of her soul
as it ascended from her dead body.

A force stopped her.

"MY DAUGHTER,
YOU HAVE BEEN BETRAYED
AND MISTREATED.

I HAVE NEED OF YOUR ENERGY.
TO REWARD YOU FOR YOUR FUTURE
DUTY, I HAVE CREATED A PARADISE
IN THE OPAL AS YOUR HOME.

WHEN THE TIME COMES,
YOU SHALL BE FREE."

"As you wish Mother.
My soul is yours to command."

And the opal absorbed her soul
with a swirl of the wind.

Azurmus bent over Mariam's body,
took her lifeless hand into his,
and pried the ring off her finger.

He swirled it in a glass of water
to clean off her blood,
then locked the ring back
into the puzzle box.

With a snap of his fingers,
a black vortex opened.

He stepped through into a crystal cave
and deposited the box
on an alabaster slab.

Nine

After passing through a small village,
I procure a pair of pack horses
to ease our legs.

With the Talisman secure in my nap-sack,
the urgency of our travel lessened.

We meander across the countryside,
through fields and over hills, journeying
towards the Keep of Our Triple Mother.

At night, we camp along the road
and Alice tells her story.

———

I am purity and a sacred vessel,
the object of dreams:
Knights quest for my pleasure
and poets sing my praises.

There have always
been three sisters
and we never age.

I am the youngest,
Anastasia is in the middle,
and Morana is the ancient one.

Our mother is time, space, and eternity.
She surrounds us and never abandons us.
Our father is the earth.

Their love affair shapes everything
and knows no bounds.

On the day I came into being,
lightning crashed and thunder bellowed
as the earth rattled.

Morana guided my previous aspect
by the hand and lead her into oblivion.
The impression of her death
still lingers in my memory.

I opened my eyes
and Anastasia greeted me
with a smile and a curtsy.

She took me by the hand
and brought me in close for a hug.
She smelled like the coming of spring
and fresh morning dew.

She went to my armoire
and dressed me
in a flowing frock
of the golden sun.

I knew that I have always loved her.

To be desired
and never to be touched
became a torture.

As I slept,
I felt my lust expand,
leave my body,
and form its own existence.

It grew into its own entity:
a being that transcended sexual identity,
a being that allowed me to act out my wants,
a being named Yssup.

Night after night, I traveled
as a disconnected passenger,
hidden in Yssup's mind.

I observed as my accumulated libido
rained over the unsuspecting residents
who lived in the Keep.

One night,
Yssup entered
Anastasia's chamber.

I fought to take hold and control him.
I could not allow my lust to ravage my sister
but I was powerless to do anything.

She must of have had a nightmare
as she was tangled up in her bed clothes
with her nightgown riding high on her thigh.

Yssup reached forward
and pushed her gown
until it was over her waist.

He leaned in
and kissed where her thighs join together,
parting her lips with his tongue.

She began to squirm
and moan as the motion intensified.
I felt Yssup harden as she ate my sister.

He moved to reposition herself
and slide in his cock;
Anastasia's eyes opened wide
in awareness.

With a guttural curse, she yelled,
"Aufhören tier!"
And with a clap of her hands,
a force wave knocked Yssup
across the room.

As he disappeared,
I awoke trembling in reaction to
what Yssup almost did to my sister.

I watched as the sun rose
and flooded my room with its light.
Anastasia soon followed to see me.

"Good morning, Alice.
I see that you are awake.

Your power has increased
as the event approaches.

I need to send you away
but only for a little while.

You will go to
the Forgotten Kingdom.

When the envoy arrives,
you will know the time
to return home has come."

I was a little scared of the unknown
but I wanted to please my sister
so I nodded slowly in agreement.

She waved both hands
in a pattern over the wall
and a portal opened before us.

I could see a tall tower standing
in the center of an open field.

"All your needs will be cared for.
I will see you again soon."

I hugged Anastasia tightly,
kissed her cheek,
and passed through the entrance.

As I glanced over my shoulder,
she blew me a kiss
and the portal snapped shut behind me.

———

Coming around a final hillock,
the towers of the Keep appear before us.
The afternoon sun reflects rainbows
from their glass windows.

We should arrive after
nightfall in time to sup.

With a burst of excitement,
Alice gives her pony a kick
to increase its speed.

Her blonde hair and clothing flow behind her.
I click my tongue twice and follow her lead.

Ten

As we travel across a stagnant moat,
I hear frogs sing in unison to the clip clop
of our horses' hooves.

The guards have seen us
and they recognize Alice for who she is.

The Keep is carved of granite mined from a local quarry
with walls stretching until they scrap the sky.
I feel the presence of an ancient and phenomenal power.

The setting sun hides behind the buildings
as an early twilight descends upon us.

A small army of retainers and footmen surrounds us.

They hold our ponies and allow us to dismount.

Alice makes her way through the open door
like a hero returning from the Crusades.

"Edwin.
Welcome to my home.

You will be led to a chamber to freshen up.
When the time arrives to meet my sister,
someone will come for you."

As I watch her walk away,
a servant motions for me to follow.

I am led from the gilded hall
to a diminutive side tunnel.

A high whisper of breeze
sneaks through the walls
and sings its song in my ears.

After journeying in a labyrinth,
we walk through a mirror's shimmer
and the servant leaves me alone.

The room is sparse like a monk's cell
with only a bed and side table
on a bare stone floor.

I splash water onto my face
and lay down to rest from our journey.

As I close my eyes, I am whisked away.

A group of women stand together in a fairy ring
holding hands and chant incantations.

They are the three who are one:

The Maiden,
The Matron,
and The Crone.

Words plummet from their mouths
like a waterfall over a cliff
becoming a defeating roar of white noise.

Fire ignites above their heads and licks the air,
burning blue in a pure cold heat.

As it expands,
mushrooming into a ball,
the flames descend,

turning the three sisters
into standing skeletons
with their hands threaded together.

A gale blows from the north creating a vortex
that pulls their dried bones up
and scatters them into the atmosphere.

Their disembodied chatting elevates an octave.

I feel liquid drip down my face
and bring my fingers to touch my ear.
They come away bloody.

The vortex of fire collapses upon its weight
and a wing'd dragon appears
like a phoenix from the ashes.

The golden eyes of the Goddess pierce my soul
and I tremble to receive the honor.

"I am Lilith, Athena, and Morgaina.
I am the power of the earth.
I am the ONE.

You have been chosen
to bring about my return.

Your life and soul belong to me."

As if from a great distance,
I hear a rhythmic beating,
faint but consistent.

"The time for you to go has arrived."

I feel my mind settle back into my body
and the comfort of my bed surrounds me.

The beating becomes clearer:
It's a firm knock on wood.

I hear a muffled voice.
"Lord Edwin,
Do you hear me?"

"Y-yes... yes.
Please enter."

The door cracks open at a glacial speed
and my guide from earlier steps in.

"The time has arrived for dinner.
I've been sent to fetch you.
I have also brought you a fresh tunic."

He holds a garment of bright marigold
with threads of white woven in a herringbone pattern.

After quickly dressing me,
we reenter the labyrinth
with him in the lead.

"What's your name, lad?"

"Lord?
I am Zön, son of Zeth."

"We are well met.
Thank you for your assistance.

What can you tell me of your mistress?"
"Lady Alice?"

"No.
Her sister who I am on the way to meet."

"My Lord,
I am proud of my work and happy to have it.
My place is not to discuss Mistress Anastasia
or her business.

You will meet her soon enough
and can form your own opinion."

"Very well.
I... I understand.
Thank you."

"You are most welcome, Lord Edwin."

As I follow the rest of the way in silence,
Zön seems to speed his step
in order to lighten his burden quicker.

He stops in front of an archway
and bows before me.

"We have arrived, my Lord.
Please enjoy your evening."

I enter the dining hall
and see Alice already sitting,
batting a grape between her hands.

She is dressed in a white satin gown
with a bow on her shoulder.

"Night greetings to you Alice.
How fairs your homecoming?"

She glares at me
and rolls her eyes.

Ignoring her mood,
I take my seat across from her
and await the arrival of her sister.

The table is a long rectangle
with places set for two other people.

Alice catches me glancing around.

"One seat is for Anastasia,
whom you will soon see,
and the other is for Morana,
my other sister.

She never joins us
but we prepare a place for her anyway."

Dinner begins with a cold soup,
but no sign of Anastasia.

"Should we wait for your sister to join us?"

"No.
You may begin.
We do not rely on old protocol here."

"Very well."

As we eat,
a minstrel recites "The Epic of Gilgamesh"
with a lute for accompaniment.

After luscious meats,
dripping melted fat and grease,
and an array of vegetables,
we partake in a firm vanilla custard.

BONG...

     BONG...

         BONG...

The tower bells ring with the coming of midnight.

As the clock's last counting resonates in my ears,
the same golden eyes from the gala
appear out of the darkened doorway
and reaffirm their hold upon me.

Her face, free from the mask,
is as I imagine in my deepest dreams:
full ruby lips captured in an oval visage.

"Lord Edwin,
Please excuse my tardiness.
I hope you have enjoyed your dinner
and Alice's company.

I am the Lady Anastasia."

Gaining my feet,
I walk over with a flourish, bow,
and present her extended hand
with a kiss.

"The pleasure is mine."

"The evening grows into morning.
It is late and we have much to discuss.
Come with me."

Alice waves goodnight with a smirk
as Anastasia takes my hand
and leads me out of the room.

Eleven

After a few twists and turns,
she guides me to her pleasure dome.

As pale flames flicker
from hanging metal cages,
crimson silk billows from the walls
with pillows strewn across the bed.

She points to an overstuffed chair.
"Sit here and wait for me,"
she says and disappears behind a three-part screen.

Each panel shows a different aspect of the Goddess:
The first panel looks like Alice with eyes of the sea,
the second, Anastasia surrounded by a golden light,
and the third shows death with a gaze of despair.

A rumble of thunder crashes
and Anastasia appears before me
wearing nothing but the ancient mists of time.

"You have completed your quest
and returned the chalice to her home.

In preparation for the Convergence,
we must join our bodies and fuse our souls."

Grabbing me by my tunic,
she pulls me forward
and brings her lips to mine.

I feel a rush of history
through her electric touch.

Kingdoms rise and fall around me
as her tongue forces its way into my mouth.

She is my air and my life.
I live for her.
I live through her.

My hands fumble over her body
unsure of their duty.

I trace the curves of her hips
and cup her butt with a tight grip.

The deposited animus of Yussp awakens
and seeps through my body
like lava flowing from a rupture.

Burning with desire,
I stand, pick her up,
and toss her on the bed.

Her tongue licks her lips
as she beckons me
with a flick of her fingers.

My entire being is engorged,
hardened and veiny.

My tunic disintegrates at my touch
and I pounce upon her,
joining my flesh to her flesh.

As I enter her valley,
a river of wetness erupts
and smooths my way.

My hips pump as I kiss her mouth
with each thrust pushing her breath into me.

Sonic booms explode
as air escapes from between
our slapping skin.

Riding a wave of ecstasy,
the pressure of our love making
builds in my loins.

Her fingers create crevices in my back
and we merge into one beast.

As Yssup takes over,
our intermingled essence releases
and mixes in the cup of her valley.

All life exits my body.

I sink into the bed
and drift into sleep,
holding Anastasia in my arms.

Twelve

It is the new moon
in the month of the Spring Equinox.

A hum of urgency courses through the castle
as the staff prepares for the evening's event.

Zön has laid out the clothes I am to wear:
a black formal dress with a white bow tie

and a hooded cloak of midnight.

I have not seen Anastasia or Alice
but I have been given specific instructions.

I dress and place the box
containing the Ring of Azurmus
into the cloak's inner pocket.

Pulling the hood over my head,
I exit my room and find Zön waiting for me.

He leads me to the court-yard where,
almost hidden in the night's darkness,
a carriage waits.

With our travel's steady rocking,
I drift into a trance-like state.
After we stop,
I return to awareness.

"We have arrived Lord Edwin.
Please stay in the cabin until you are called."

I look out the window
and notice, through lighted torches,
we are on the precipice of a scar in the earth.

Three figures stand out
as they journey the carved pathway
into the deep crevice.

The first two wear matching hoods,
which glow in their whiteness.
The third is the vagueness of shadows.

In the center of the quarry,
a fairy ring burns in colorful flames
with a pentagram laid out in the center.

This is a night of powerful magick.
Maybe a summoning...

Part 2

The High Priestess

THE HIGH PRIESTESS

One

In the cold midnight of the new year,
the time of divining has arrived.
We must see what the future holds.

As the sun holds its reign in the sky,
Alice goes into the stable
and handpicks our offering.

An undersized sheep
with a dirty white coat
is chosen to be honored.

The stable boys have sheared her clean
and have conducted a ritual bath.

In the center of a field,
a scribed circle in the dead grass
glistens with frost.

Dancing torch flames illumine
our path from the Keep
and surround our destination.

The ewe, tied to a stake in the center,
bleats out its nervous welcome.

We carry our needed implements:
Alice has a wooden bowl,
Morana swings a sickle sharpened to a sheen,
and I hold my grimoire.

Turning to the appropriate page,
I begin the ceremony.

"Mother of all!
We call to you and sing your praises.
We ask for your guidance."

Morana stands ready,
her blade at the sheep's throat.
Alice holds the bowl underneath.

"We offer a sacrifice of innocence
as the price for your knowledge."

Morana is quick and efficient.
The ewe's scream drowns
in the rush of its blood.

Alice fills the void
by keeping the bowl
in the steaming stream.

The lamb falls to the ground.

I take the bowl from Alice
and hold it above my head.

"As I baptize myself in this living liquid,
take over my vision
and allow me to see what I must."

Sticky blood drenches my body.

Morana has the sheep on its back
and swiftly pulls out the entrails.
The smell of offal drifts in the air.

I fall to my knees and plunge in my arms.
The gore coats up to my elbows.
My hands examine our future in the guts.

I feel light rush around me
and have a moment of insight.

**"After discovering him among Society,
Death will nearly devour you.
Purity becomes stained with passion,
which will be injected into the one who finds her.
The Convergence brings union and justice."**

The world shifts to black around me
and I collapse to the ground.

I hear Morana's voice echo
as if from a great distance.

"Take Mistress Anastasia to the Keep,
have a handmaiden bathe her
and put her to bed.

Alice. Go with them.

You must stay by your sister's side.
She needs rest after her ordeal.

I will see you when I can."

Two

With a dream's mist surrounding me,
I reach out to the left and to the right.
The walls feel of slime.

A continual drip falls from above
and a plop sounds below.

Drip, plop!
  Drip, plop!
    Drip, plop!

A rumble of angry voices echoes
as their shouts float down the tunnel.

I thought I eluded them.
I must be so very careful
to not draw their attention.

Pushing myself forward faster
and trying not to slosh or create waves,
I move through the darkness.

Water weighs the hem of my dress
and my shoes are bogged down.

With a
　　　splash,
I trip, tumble, and fall head first.
The flowing stream runs over me.

"Oy! What's that?
I think she's this way!"

The round whiteness of lamps bounce
as my pursuers run towards me.

They close off any chance of escape.

Arms wrap like tangled bed clothes
as my skirt rides high on my thigh.

The mist engulfs me.
Goosebumps emerge with a chill
as my naked sex becomes exposed.

Hands spread my legs apart
and hug over my hips.

I gasp as a throbbing tongue parts my lips.
My nightmare of pursuit expands
and turns into a vision of pleasure.

I give myself over to ecstasy
and allow each thrusting kiss
to radiate through my body.

Their force vibrates my larynx
causing a slow moan to build
into a crescendo.

Reaching between my legs,
I hold the phantom mouth
on the right place.

As my body hurls towards its little death,
the being moves to reposition itself.

The dream dissipates as my eyes open
to the feeble light of my chamber.

A brute of hideous beauty
stands between my legs,
ready to impale me on its shaft.

I look into its face
and see Alice's eyes stare back.

I clap my hands with a guttural curse
and exclaim, "Aufhören tier!"
I then hurl a force wave to knock the beast
across the room into a wall.

I spring out of my night nest,
hurry to where the creature lies crumpled,
and watch it slowly disappear.

With the crisis averted,
I am aware of what has invaded us.

Alice developed a succubus
to act out her emerging desires.

Slinking back into bed,
I slide into my covers,
and hope to reenter sleep's fortress.

On the morrow,
Alice must be sent
to a place of containment.

Three

With the ruby wax seal over
the parchment's slit broken,
the invitation lies where I dropped it.

December 20, 18—
The Society invites you to
celebrate the Winter Solstice.
Join us at our Gala!
Please RSVP.

As a member of Magick's upper echelon,
I must make an appearance.

In the Keep's highest tower,
I stand below its open roof
and look into the night.

The distant stars twinkle
in the moonless sky.

In the corner, covered in dust,
an ancient loom waits to be needed.

(It had an important role in another story,
but that will not be told here.)

With a tug and a pull,
I move the loom into the center
of the exposed room.

Reaching into the atmosphere,
I grab a gathering of night filament
and tie it to the spindle.

As I mutter a short incantation, I pierce my finger:
A blood sacrifice on the needle's sharpened point.

With a rocking of the foot petal
and a spinning of the wheel,
I pull fabric made of sparkling darkness.

Constellations expand, collapse, and implode
as I run my hand along the folds.
A universal power rumbles beneath my touch.

My seamstress will fashion
the bolt into a form fitting flowing gown.

To conceal myself in the masquerade,
I have procured a vizard:
Sea-foam feathers plume around
frozen porcelain features.
The lips form into a forever pout.

My spirit-sisters on the coast
summoned Neptune and used his trident
and the ancient charm of making
to fashion the mask from the churning ocean.

I can taste the sea salt
and hear the crying of gulls
when my face is hidden by the facade.

"Exhale, Madam!"

Each pull of the corset's ribbon
straightens my back
and pushes out my air.

The whale bones
sculpt my torso
into an hourglass.

I feel the flow of time
as necessary events fall into place.

Gazing at myself in a full-length mirror,
I see a majestic creature brimming
with mystic energy.

Feeling confident and beautiful,
I leave for the Gala
and the fulfillment of destiny.

After exiting my carriage,
I climb the crimson-carpeted steps.

A multitude of lilies, hibiscus, and orchids—
flowers born in a hothouse—
funnel the arriving guests towards the hall.

My eyes water from their aroma.

Hanging from the rafters,
tapestries of conquered banner-men
tell the story of their defeat.

Our host hails from an ancient family
built upon rivers of gore.

In my full regalia,
I hand my card to the footman.

He bows before me
and announces to all present,
"The Lady Anastasia of Our Triple Mother!"

With my shoulders held back
and my eyes looking forward,
I stroll into the chamber.

The multitude greets me
with flourishes, whispers, and murmurs.
Respect and fear exudes from their pores.

The room is draped with flowing silks
and heavily upholstered furniture.
The color of dried blood prevails.

A pendulum clock
reaches towards the high ceiling
with a face of Cyrillic runes.

The minutes swing away
as a spring stores energy
for the chiming of the bells.

As I flitter and float around the various guests,
like a bumble bee to blooming buds,

the torrent of conversation engulfs me
in its mumble and hum.

Tick-tock!
      Tick-tock!
            Tick-tock!
                  Tick-tock!

We wait with nervous anticipation
for the coming of midnight.

At the moment of the first toll's peal,
I glance across the room
and our gazes meet.

His harried countenance
is highlighted by a well-trimmed beard
and swept-back chestnut hair.

My image reflects in the sky of his eyes.

I open my arms in greeting
and, as a river rushes down an incline,
he flows across the room.

His embrace envelopes me in calm comfort.

With a muffled hum,
my voice vibrates through the mask:

"The time of the Convergence has arrived.
Search for the Talisman and you shall find me."

With the twelfth sounding
still echoing around the chamber,
I slip from his grasp
and merge into the room of revelers.

He stands slightly dazed
with a glazed look in his eyes.

As he makes his way towards a pair of French doors,
I steal away and leave the Gala.

With a rush of mobility,
I run down the hallway,
past the flowers,
and out the great door.

In time with my decent from the final step,
my driver pulls into place.

Locking the door latch behind me,
I settle into the cushioned bench
while the outside scenery flies into a blur.

The prophecy of the New Year
has been set into motion.

 *five*

With a silent whoosh,
I feel my body slip away.
The weight of mortality
no longer holds me prisoner.

In the twilight of dawn's birth,
I look down to discover
my carriage covered
under loosened hard pack.

My driver scrambles
down the mountain side,
working his way to my aid.

Off in the distance,
a beacon of pulsating rhythm
vibrates across the atmosphere.

Lub-dub.
        Lub-dub.
                Lub-dub.

With the speed of thought,
I appear at a great estate.
Deer prance over the grounds.

I am drawn into the manor house,
float through the walls,
and appear in his chamber.

Tangled in bed clothes,
he tosses and turns
through the coil of sleep.

I descend from the ceiling,
merge my hands with his head,
and plug into his consciousness.

I have become the universe,
the everlasting Mother,
the secret to existence.

Words pour from my mouth
in the voice of another:

**"Impale yourself on the Spear of Desire
and bring me the Chalice of Life.
Only then you shall be worthy and free."**

The elastic grasp of my body to my soul springs back
and I am launched away from the hidden Chalet.

"Mistress Anastasia.
Can you hear me?"

As my eyes open,
I feel the cold snow chill my bones.

A trench created by my body
drags away from the carriage.

"Yes, Charles.
I hear you."

"We've been caught in an avalanche.
I was thrown free and one of the horses broke away.

We are not far from the Keep.

After I build a fire to warm you,
I will wrangle our loose friend,
and we will make our way home."

"Very good.
Thank you."

 Six

I do not remember having a childhood.
I remember being as I am.

Flashes of my past existence populate my memories.

I have always fulfilled my function.

Like the sun in the sky,
I seem eternal.
But in the course of forever,
I am finite.

I take the major arcana into hand
and spread a tarot reading.

The first pass:
The High Priestess. The Empress. Death.

My sisters and I always appear first.
I am the Priestess,
Alice is the Empress,
and Morana is always Death.

Leaving Death alone,
I pick up the Priestess and the Empress
and lay them side by side.

I deal three more cards.

The Tower lays below the Empress
with the Lovers below the High Priestess.
The Magician bridges between them.

THE LOVERS.

He saves my sister from the tower
and becomes my lover.

What happens next?

I peal a single card:
The Wheel of Fortune.

The time has arrived to assemble the players.
I place the High Priestess, the Empress, and Death
above the wheel with the Magician below.

I am missing one arm of the pentacle.

I draw from the deck:
The Hanged Man.

With the placing of this card,
the pentagram is complete.
The ritual may commence.

I shuffle the deck three times
and the World, the Mother Goddess,
reveals herself.

I stack my sisters and I into one pile
and place the World on top.
We have evolved beyond our mortal selves.

For what reason do we gather?

Two more cards:
The Devil. Justice.

I place the Devil on the Wheel
and lay Justice over him.

Our Mother brings a reckoning.

As wind gusts through the window,
a bolt of lightning strikes in the courtyard.
The cards catch on the breeze and flutter about.

I frantically slap at them
and secure a few to the table.

Death, the Magician, the High Priestess
and the Empress lay disarrayed in my grasp.
The rest, having served their purpose, blow away.

The final draw:
The Sun. The Fool.

Happiness and joy abound,
the scales are balanced,
and everything is reset.

Seven

Around one hundred years ago,
the conditions were ripe
(as they are now)
for the coming of our Mother.

Our little sister had been sent
to the Forgotten Kingdom
to await the arrival of a champion.
Unfortunately, he was not pure of heart.

I awoke in the middle of the night
and knew something was amiss.

After creating a portal
with a swipe of my hands,
I stepped through
and saw the fiend scurrying away.

Out of the corner of my eye,
a crumpled figure lay
with its arms and legs akimbo.

Pulling power from the moon,
I threw a lightning cage
and captured the one trying to escape.

To confirm my suspicions,
I hurried to the base of the tower
and found Alice's predecessor,
a cracked chalice leaking her life's liquid.

I fought the urge to rend my clothing
and celebrate my burgeoning grief.
Justice must be extracted.

A flick of my wrist
bought the prison
and its occupant to me.

Dolor weighed heavily upon my heart
as I began the interrogation.

With a gesture towards the broken mass, I asked:
"My sister's blood fertilizers the soil.
Can you tell me how this occurred?"

His skin was paper white
as he shivered with fear.
He could see the calm fury
burn in my eyes.

"After coming upon this tower
and being captured by the beast,
her beauty enraptured me.

As she nursed me back to health,
a confused sensation of lust and love
flowed through my body.

I knew that I had to have her.

We spent days running
through various rooms
and trying secret doors.

I would steal glances
and fugitive touches.

The feel of her pulse echoed
and madness soon engulfed me.

As we stood together at the top of the tower,
overlooking the surrounding landscape,
I skated my fingers along her back,
following the crevice of her spine.

The heat of her flesh radiated
through her clothing
and drove my inhibitions away.

I wrapped her in my arms
and turned her to face me.
Kissing hard, I pushed my lips into hers.

She struggled to break my grasp
but I kept her immobile in my grip.

With pressure and pain,
fire sprouted in my groin,
burnt its way through my stomach,
and radiated over my body.

The force of her knee
drained the strength from my arms
and she slipped away.

I staggered after her.

As time slowed to a crawl,
my vision shrank to a myopic focus:
Her beauty's radiance filled my world.

With a fateful lunge,
I threw myself at her,
and knocked her over the edge.
My sun plummeted towards the earth.

I could hear the crush of flesh
bounce off the wall
until a hollow
        splat
echoed in my ears.

The realization of what I did
descended upon me in a cold emptiness.

Bile traveled up my throat
and I spewed over the cool flagstone roof.

I did not mean to kill her.
I... I only wanted to love her."

He ended his narrative
with a forlorn look in his eyes.

With a snap of my fingers,
his cage dissolved,
and I opened my arms to him.

"I understand and I forgive you."

As I held him in a motherly embrace,
his tears poured over my bosom.

My personal grief began to take hold
and I sobbed along with him.

After a few tender moments,
I whispered in his ear:
"Will you forgive me for my vengeance?"

He looked me in the eye,
slightly confused.
"Wha... "
My dagger,
entering from under his ribs
and slid into his heart.

A trickle of blood seeped
from the corner of his mouth
and I held him until his lingering life left
before gently laying him to the ground.

Eight

"Anastasia.
I have come."

I opened my eyes
and looked for the disembodied voice.
Morana had appeared to fulfill her function.

She reached into the mass of mangled flesh
and clasped the spirit hand of the soul within.

She acted as the midwife
and helped our sister's essence
to shuffle off the shell of her mortal coil.

Swirls of color danced before me.
My eyes had to squint against
the blinding beauty of her afterlife.

Cradling the infant spirit in her arms,
the duo began to ascend into the sky
following a spiraling core into the stratosphere.

Morana looked down at me.
"Go home and wait for our sister."

They both twinkled out of existence
in between the blinks of my eyes,
leaving me alone with the fallen champion.

At their exit,
the Forgotten Kingdom
began to rattle and deteriorate.

I swiped my hands through the air
and mumbled an opening spell.

A portal back to The Keep appeared
and I stepped across the threshold
into our shared home.

Nine

After waiting through a period of gestation,
our youngest aspect rejoined us.

As heavy clouds bellowed,
a great rain washed over the earth
with lightning exploding across the sky.

The servants wailed
as if the ground would open up
and swallow them whole.

I sat cross-legged in my chamber
holding the lotus position
with my hands out before me.

I pushed my consciousness into the universe
to create a path for my sister's essence to follow.

The music of the elder planets
transmitted along my wavelength into my core.
The night songs of Jupiter and Saturn
brought a vibration of peace and calm.

As my thoughts drifted,
she caught hold of me
and plummeted towards earth

like Lucifer falling from Heaven.

My vocal cords became hers
and we screamed with the terror
of becoming corporal.

As my hands clenched into fists,
my nails dug into my palms,
baptizing my arms in blood.

"Mother!
Bring our pain to an end!"

The room around me went black
as all thoughts and feelings stopped
and I collapsed to the floor.

Warmth spread over my body
and over my face.

I saw the sun glow red
through the capillaries of my eyelids.
The bird's song echoed in my ears
from the tree outside the window.

I opened my eyes
and a fresh morning greeted me.

Peeling myself off the floor,
I pulled myself to my feet.

With a stagger over to the water pitcher,
I poured the clear liquid into a bowl,
splashed my face,
and unbloodied my arms.

I let my soiled night clothes slip to the floor,
draped a fresh robe over my person,
and left the chamber.

After coming upon my sister's closed door,
I leaned against it,
felt the course wood under my fingers,
and gathered my strength.

I held my breath
and slowly pushed open the door.

My little sister,
who was recently lost,
lay on her bed twitching in a dream.

I stifled a cry of joy.
I did not want to disturb her,
but I was too late.

She opened her eyes.

I greeted her with a smile
and gave a curtsy.

As I sat on her bed,
I cradled her hand in mine
and brought her close for a hug.

We stayed that way for a number of heart beats.

"Let us get you ready to face the world."

I went to the armoire
and after a brief search,
dressed her in a flowing frock
of golden sun.

Ten

I hear the whispering of nature
and know of their travels.

After leaving the Forgotten Kingdom,
Alice and her champion secure the Talisman,
and she leads him to me.

I long for our promised connection.

A tremble courses over my skin
as I imagine his touch:
calloused hands caressing.

With dust particles dancing
in an early afternoon beam,
I slip out of my robe.

The bath seeps steam
from the edges of a copper basin
as a slight fire smolders below.

When I slide into the tub,
the water's tension is disturbed
freeing the trapped rose oil.

My nostrils are perfumed
and I absorb the scent.

A towel pillows beneath my head
as I close my eyes
and wander in my thoughts.

Life's stress leaves with each breath.

My wayward hands trace over my curves
exploring my wilderness,
only to settle in my valley.

I caress the folds,
slide a finger in my gateway,
and fondle my pleasure button.
It feels of smooth velvet.

I tease myself
but do not want to finish.
I need my blood to boil with desire.

In this state of almost ecstasy,
my spirit lifts and transcends.

I feel our Mother
take me into her bosom
and hold me tight.

**"You will become electric.
You will be a super nova.
You will be the Light."**

Knock!
       KNOCK!

I am brought back to myself
by a sharp double rap.

I notice that the fire has burnt out.
The water grows cool
and surrounds me in a liquid cocoon.

A muffled
    "Madame?"
        sounds.

"Entrez s'il vous plait."

The door creaks open
and Elaine shuffles into my chamber.

"Yes.
What news?"

"Mademoiselle Alice has returned home
along with a... un compagnon."

"Excellente!
She will come to me presently.
Make sure our guest is taken care of."

"Oui Madame."

As the door clicks closed,
I bolt from the tub and in my haste,
water droplets spray across the room.

I grab a fresh silk robe
embroidered with spring flowers
and enclose it around myself.

Sitting in front of my dressing table,
I untie my hair and let it drape loose.
A boar bristle brush straightens the ringlets.

As the steady strokes settle my excitement,
the rhythmic motion brings a song to mind.

With my eyes closed,
I hum until the words take over
and pour from my lips.

At the beginning of the second chorus,
a sweet high voice doubles the lyrics.

I open my eyes and see Alice reflected
in the mirror with a large-spread smile.

Emitting a squee, I jump up
and wrap her in my arms.

She smells of road dust, sweat, and sunshine.
I feel her heart almost beat out of her chest.

"My darling sister!
Welcome home!
Tell me of your adventure."

Eleven

Before the sun rises,
I disentangle myself from Edwin
and slink out of the chamber.

My mind feels overwhelmed
with throbbing pleasure radiating
between my core and my follicles.

I wallow in the endorphins
and reflect on the previous evening.

With crippling self-doubt,
I stood at the edge of the dining hall.
The wall felt cool as it lended me its support.

Was I worthy of this great responsibility?

I closed my eyes
and whispered a petite prayer.

The Goddess answered
by straightening my back
and lifting my chin.

I am Her fierce warrior!
My strength is limitless!

I can do anything!

The chiming of midnight began,
and I timed my breathing with each Bong!

As the final ringing resonated,
I felt at peace and relaxed enough
to step through the doorway.

Our eyes drew together
and locked into place.

I did not recognize
the words of introduction
that poured from my mouth,

but I could feel
the flow of our essence
join in the open air.

He rose from the table
and came towards me.

Electricity sparked
as his hand slipped
into my waiting one.
He branded it with a kiss.

As Ariadne helped Theseus
to navigate the labyrinth,
I guided Edwin to my pleasure dome.

Twelve

After resting from my night's exertions,
I break my fast on kitchen scraps
before meeting my sisters.

Among the color and scent of summer plants,
I find them huddled in the conservatory
whispering secrets.

With a sparkle in her eye,
Alice greets me.

"Hullo, sweet sister!
I trust your conversation
with Edwin was enlightening."

Ignoring her completely
I direct my response to Morana.

"Is everything prepared for this evening?"

"Yes.

The staff has their orders
and we are ready."

"Very good."

Using a pair of shears,
I snip a black orchid from its stem
and place it in a mortar.

I slowly grid the flower with a pestle
to create a pulpy mash.

Three crystal flutes with sterling rims
and stems stand waiting.

I place the orchard mixture
at the bottom of each glass
and, after popping a cork on a bottle,
I top them off with Rosé.

I present each of my sisters with a drink
and hold mine up in tribute.

"This symbolizes the strength
of our joining and power of our bond.

It is the day of the new moon
in the month of the Spring Equinox.
The time of Convergence has arrived."

Part 3

The World

THE WORLD.

One

We watch from the bell tower.
Mistress Morana has summoned us
as a silent witness to tonight's happening.

We manifest on this plane as ravens;
creatures with black silky feathers
that ripple in the light breeze.

There are five of us:
One for each of the principal players.
One for each point of the Pentacle.
One hive mind among us.

The three sisters exit the Keep first
and board the waiting carriage.

The youngest in pure white,
the middle draped in eggshell,
and the eldest as the shadow of death.

Our corresponding number joins them
as they travel to the holy site.

Edwin, guided by Zön, finally makes his way out.

We find a pocket of air,
soar on our wings, and follow him
as he journeys to the quarry.

Two

As I approach the circle,
a feeling of foreboding presses upon me.
Each sister stands on a point of the Pentacle,
leaving two empty.

"Lord Edwin,
we have brought you to participate
in our becoming.

Are you prepared to witness?"

"Yes Mistress Anastasia.
I am here to do your bidding."

"Have you brought the Ring of Azurmus?"

Reaching into my cloak pocket,
I open the box and lift it with both hands,
showing the ring to all present.

"Set the box into the circle's center
and take your place on an empty point."

I do as she asked
and move to my position.

"Morana, my eldest sister
and death's concubine,
we must complete the circle.

One thousand years ago,
as her life was stolen from her,
Queen Mariam was placed inside this ring.
Call forth our final player."

She steps forward
and pushes back her hood.
Her flesh has withered on her face,
tightening over her skull.

Her eyes seem to be empty sockets
that burn with a forbidding fire.
Long unbound hair the color of ash
streams from her head.

After screaming at the new moon,
she begins the incantation.

"I call forth our lost sister,
Queen of the Danakil Desert,
to return to the realm of waking.
The time of your purpose has arrived."

As she speaks,
she dances around the box,
her cloak flowing with a rustle of fabric.
She pulls her hands from the earth
towards the inky expanse of sky.

The ring's stone glows like a full moon
as a figure materializes to my right,
filling in the final pentagram point.

Three

In the peak of the day's heat,
the trees feed of the spring's pure waters
as I lay in their shade.

I do not remember how I came to be here
but I do remember violence and pain.

This is the oasis of the Goddess.
She provides for my wants and my desires.

As I feel the sting of hunger rumble my stomach,
a servant appears carrying a tray
consisting of cut fruit and sweetmeats.

I select a plump orange
that glistens with its refreshing nectar.

After testing its fragile fibers with my tongue,
I tear my teeth into its flesh
and swallow the juice and pulp.

I let the emptied rind slip
from my hand
and fall to the ground.

With a quick survey
of the manna before me,
I make a new choice.

"Feed me the sugary confection."

Akeem picks up the pastry
between his thumb and forefinger
and guides it into my mouth.

I taste the sweetness of the cake
along with something more primal.

Taking his hand in mine,
I guide his extended finger
back into my mouth
and run my tongue along its coarseness.

A new hunger ignites in my loins.

"You look as if you need to eat.
You must feed from my cup of life."

A smile spreads over his face.
"As you wish, my Queen."

With a practiced flick of his wrist,
he pulls the tie of my robe
and frees my skin from the cloth.

My downy body hair stands at attention
as the desert breeze blows its warm breath.

His lips attach to my nipple
and he coaxes my blood into hardness.

He tastes the skin across my stomach
and travels through the forest of my mons.

As he parts my lips and enters inside me,
I spread my legs to ease his journey.

Through slotted lids, I watch his head bob
as his tongue slurps at my velvet nub.

I lose touch of all reality
and travel to a realm of intensity.

Using my hands,
I hold his head
and grind on his face.

I feel the river of life flow out of me
as I buck and moan.

Pleasure's pressure builds
and needs a further release.

"Fuck me!"

He springs up, wipes his chin,
and enters my flesh cave with molten rock.

My guts displace
as each ramming thrust
pounds into me.

I wrap my legs around him,
claw at his back,
and hold him tight.

My tongue explores his mouth
in time to his rhythmic movement.

I feel my entire body let go with a shutter
that causes my brain to become numb.

He bellows an exhausted grunt
and slumps over me.

We drift to nirvana
and float into the filament,
an entangled mess.

The speed of our ascent increases
and the coolness of the atmosphere
replaces the warmth of the desert.

Sensual sweat transforms into icy crystals.

**"THE TIME OF MY BECOMING HAS ARRIVED.
I CALL YOU BACK TO THE LIVING."**

As I look below me,
the earth has transformed into a white glow
and, because I feel frightened,
I try to hold Akeem tighter.

His once succulent flesh transforms into a mist
and I drift through him.

I am a comet barreling across the sky
heading towards oblivion.

VA-BOOM!

I shatter the celestial dome
and emerge in a darkened quarry
trapped in a circle of binding.

The sky is pitch black
and the area is lit by torches.

Four people stand on a star point with joined hands,
waiting for me to complete the connection.

I grasp the extended hands
and feel an all-encompassing energy.

"Hail Queen Mariam!
Welcome to our Passion play
and the coming of the Goddess."

After the return of the Queen,
I look to my right and see Alice.
Her face beams with a smile.

She is the rising sun
when compared to Morana's night.
I am the twilight in between.

We are three aspects of one whole.

"The circle is now complete.
Tonight is the time of joining and justice.

Queen Mariam and Edwin release our hands
but do not leave the circle.

The time of Convergence has arrived."

Alice lets go of my hand,
and I notice a swirling around the new moon.
A Stygian cloud rotates as it descends.

The triumvirate before me
continues their manual connection
as the celestial ether surrounds them.

The three sisters disappear into the fallen sky.

A beam of pure white
shoots from the new moon
into the darkened mass.

My eyes water from the intense light
but I cannot turn away.

An agonizing shriek,
composed of all their voices,
reverberates around the quarry walls
and settles in my ears.

As the powdery soot-like substance settles,
the whiteness rearranges their three forms into one
and creates a new entity.

Before me stands a being that
encompasses all womanhood.
The epitome of beauty.

She exudes an aura
of pure love and unabated lust.

She is every race
with every color hair.
Her body is perfect
but indescribable.

I feel the need to protect
and conquer her.

Flames drift from her gaze
as her eyes find mine.

I feel her fire burn my soul
and I am forever marked.

She is the Goddess!

Six

Overwhelmed by the enormity of her presence,
I break from my place in the pentacle
and fall upon my knees.

"Eternal mother,
I am humbled to serve you.
Pray tell me your name
so I may worship correctly."

**"My names are legion.
Cerdwin, Lilith, and Abra are among them
but you may call me...
Anna."**

I taste the shape of the letters
as my tongue forms the sacred word.

"Anna."

Out of the corner of my eye,
the Ring of Azurmus glistens
with a flicker of the torch lights.

Reaching without averting my gaze,
I pluck the ring from its enclosure
and hold it towards her.

"As a token of my devotion,
let me bind myself to you
and install this ring upon your finger."

"Edwin, I accept you."
She presents her left hand to me.

As I hold it steady,
the spark of her spirit flows through
the contact of our skin.

"With this sigil,
I join myself to you.
I forsake all to follow your guidance.
May you be my peace."

As I slide on the ring,
it forms to the correct size
and I am flooded with yearning.

"Thank you, Edwin."

She assists me to my feet,
wraps her arms around me in a tight hug,
and whispers in my ear.

"I am yours."

After she releases me,
I stagger back to my abandoned position
dazed from my experience.

Seven

**"Mariam. After your death,
I held your spirit from nirvana
for a future purpose.**

That time have arrived!

**Tonight, we use your energy
to call Azurmus to justice
for your mistreatment."**

We follow Anna's lead
and raise our arms to the sky.

"Demon of the deep pit,
I wear your creation
and feel your essence flow.

We summon you.

Join us in this circle,
your temporary prison.

Come to us as we chant your name."

In unison, we speak.
Each wave of words grows louder
and more assertive.

"Azurmus.
　　　Azurmus!
　　　　　AZURMUS!"

"We demand your presence!
Come to us now!"

Cr-ACK!

A bolt of lightning strikes,
and the air's filament tears asunder
above the center of our pentagram.

As an unholy birth,
a creature is pushed through the crevasse
along with lava and sulfur
to collapse upon the ground.

A tremor courses over its body
as it huddles in a fetal position.

Scaled skin reflects maroon
and steams smoke into the chill air.

There is a nub of a tail
and hooves for feet.

Moans of pain escape from its mouth
as the being gains its footing
and stands before us.

"By what are you called?"

*"I am the creator of talismans
and the curator of the mystic.*

I am Azurmus!"

THE DEVIL .

Eight

"Why have you brought me to this plane?"

A deafening silence surrounds us
as Azurmus' question hangs in the air.

A look of raging terror festers on Mariam's face.
Anna is calm and collected.

She holds her hand towards him
and splays her fingers.

"Do recognize this ring?"

A toothy smiles grows over his face.
Pointed teeth like a picket fence line his mouth.

"I crafted it after Queen Mariam summoned me.
She did not understand the true cost of my creation.

I considered letting her keep the ring,
but I am always too possessive of my work.
Everything I fashion exists with parts of my being.

To hold my power and strength,
I must keep what I produce."

"Since you are a demon,
I cannot fault you for being true to your nature,
but I will not let you be free!

I protect and avenge my own.

The time has arrived for you to answer
for the life you ended."

Anna forms a fist with her hand
and shoves the gem
into the forehead of Azurmus.

At the contact point,
burning flesh singes the air.

He howls in pain and
pulls her wrist with both his hands
as he tries to distance himself.

The bond will not break.

"Azurmus! Enter the stone!"

With a high-pitch whine,
air rushes around us
and he is absorbed.

The light of the moon
radiates from Anna's being.
It is brightest surrounding her fist.

Beginning at his feet,
Azurmus' body shrivels with a crackle
as the ring drinks his essence.

A ball of wind swirls around us
before picking up his husk
and carrying it away.

"It is done."

Nine

**"Queen Mariam.
Do you see the star left of the new moon?"**

Mariam's gaze follows the length of Anna's arm
and is guided by her pointer finger.

"Yes."

"This is where I shall bring you.
A place of peace.
A place of light.
A place of eternal reward."

Anna opens her arms wide.

"Come and embrace me."

With tears streaming down her face,
Mariam rushes to Anna
and is enclosed in her hug.

The star appears to increase in size
as if approaching the earth.

I must squint my eyes to fulfill my duty
and witness the event.

They are engulfed in its light;
a dull darkness surrounded by brightness.

Sonic rings radiate from the core
and knock me off my feet.

As I sit up on the dirt,
the ball of light contracts into the ground
and launches into space.

I follow the contrails as it travels
to its home in the sky.

Anna and Mariam have left this realm.

Ten

I gain my feet and rush over.

Crowded on the scorched earth,
three figures lay disheveled
with their limbs intertwined.

The three sisters are together.

I kneel beside Anastasia
and take up her hand.

The Ring of Azurmus glistens on her finger.

Her pulse murmurs through her wrist
and her breathing is shallow.

I lean to her ear and whisper.
"Mistress, I will take care of you."

I lift Anastasia
and motion with a nod of my head
for her footmen to follow with her sisters.

"Place Alice and Morana into their carriage
and follow me back to the Keep.
We must attend to their needs."

Once inside my carriage,
I let Anastasia's head rest on my lap
as I stoke her hair.

The wind whistles through the window
as the pitch black scenery bleeds past in a blur.

"The Goddess lives within you
and you have my devotion."

Eleven

Edwin rushes the sisters back to the Keep,
and we take to the air.

Our time of witness is complete.

Although the principal players now number four,
the five of us have seen

and will remember.

We alight from the sky into the bell tower
and await Mistress Morana's pleasure.

Epilogue

As I walk into the kitchen,
a boy sits at the table
with his eyes searching.
He holds a missive in both hands.

"Good evening to you lad.
I am Anastasia.
What is your name?"

He quickly stands to attention
and gives me a slight bow.

"I am Rodrick.
I've come in the service of Lord Edwin.
He asked for this letter to be delivered.

I arrived to the servant entra ..."

He trails off as I hold up my hand
to halt his verbal nervousness.

"We are well-met my boy.
Forget what you have heard
and do not be afraid."

I open my palm for the letter.

"You have done Edwin proud
and completed his task.

You shall stay the night, eat,
and be comfortable."

A smile spreads over his face.
"Thank you, Mistress.
You are overly kind."

"I shall pen a response
for your return on the morrow.
Good night to you."

His heels click together
as I leave the room.

I retire to my sitting room
and break the wax seal.

As I trace the quill scratches on the paper,
I devour the ink with my eyes
and feel the passion of Edwin's words.

I picture his hands as he holds the paper
and caress the feathery nib.

A veil of contentment covers me
and I feel our connection.

WHEEL ᴼꜰ FORTUNE.

Acknowledgments

I would like to thank the following people:

Manuela Serra Book Cover Design

Eva Zen Editing and Critique

Olivia and Anna for their support and feedback

About the Author

Andrew Chiniche has lived in Hawaii, the Virgin Islands, and Florida, but his favorite place is in the worlds of books and movies. He believes every work of fiction contains truth hidden in the wonderful and fantastic.

Andrew received a degree in English Literature from Mississippi State University, and currently lives in Alabama.

His previous poetry collections are "Love's Dawn" and "Gaze the Moon".

CPSIA information can be obtained
at www.ICGtesting.com
Printed in the USA
LVHW111759010420
651902LV00010B/70

9 781732 682481